DEMO SUBJECT

NOTHING

Chapter 1: Introduction

Explanation of the importance of Facebook Ads and Automation

Brief overview of the book's content

Chapter 2: Understanding Facebook Ads

Basics of Facebook Ads

Types of Facebook Ads

Setting up a Facebook Ads Account

Targeting and Ad Placement

Chapter 3: Creating Effective Facebook Ads

Creating Ad Copy and Visuals

Creating Landing Pages

A/B Testing and Optimization

Strategies for Increasing Click-Through-Rates (CTR) and Conversion Rates

Chapter 4: Facebook Ads Automation

Importance of Facebook Ads Automation

Setting up Automated Ads

Strategies for Optimizing Automated Ads

Overview of Facebook Ads Manager and Automated Rules

Chapter 5: Measuring and Analyzing Facebook Ads Performance

Metrics to track for Facebook Ads

Interpreting Facebook Ads Analytics

Creating Custom Reports

Chapter 6: Advanced Facebook Ads Strategies

Remarketing and Retargeting

Lookalike Audiences

Campaign Budget Optimization

Scaling and Expanding Facebook Ad Campaigns

Chapter 7: Facebook Ads Case Studies

Examples of successful Facebook Ad campaigns

Analysis of the strategies used in each campaign

Chapter 8: Facebook Ads Troubleshooting

Common Facebook Ads issues and how to troubleshoot them

Chapter 9: Conclusion

Recap of key points

Final thoughts on Facebook Ads and Automation.

In this book, we will explore the world of Facebook Ads and Automation, and how you can use these powerful tools to grow your business. We will start with the basics of Facebook Ads, including the different types of ads and how to set up a Facebook Ads account. From there, we will move on to creating effective Facebook ads, including strategies for creating compelling ad copy and visuals

Contents

Foreword

Scaling and Expanding Facebook Ad Campaigns

Chapter 7: Facebook Ads Case Studies

Examples of successful Facebook Ad campaigns

Analysis of the strategies used in each campaign

Chapter 8: Facebook Ads Troubleshooting

Common Facebook Ads issues and how to troubleshoot them

Chapter 9: Conclusion

Recap of key points

Final thoughts on Facebook Ads and Automation.

In this book, we will explore the world of Facebook Ads and Automation, and how you can use these powerful tools to grow your business. We will start with the basics of Facebook Ads, including the different types of ads and how to set up a Facebook Ads account. From there, we will move on to creating effective Facebook ads, including strategies for creating compelling ad copy and visuals

Preface

Scaling and Expanding Facebook Ad Campaigns

Chapter 7: Facebook Ads Case Studies

Examples of successful Facebook Ad campaigns

Analysis of the strategies used in each campaign

Chapter 8: Facebook Ads Troubleshooting

Common Facebook Ads issues and how to troubleshoot them

Chapter 9: Conclusion

Recap of key points

Final thoughts on Facebook Ads and Automation.

In this book, we will explore the world of Facebook Ads and Automation, and how you can use these powerful tools to grow your business. We will start with the basics of Facebook Ads, including the different types of ads and how to set up a Facebook Ads account. From there, we will move on to creating effective Facebook ads, including strategies for creating compelling ad copy and visuals

Acknowledgements

Scaling and Expanding Facebook Ad Campaigns

Chapter 7: Facebook Ads Case Studies

Examples of successful Facebook Ad campaigns

Analysis of the strategies used in each campaign

Chapter 8: Facebook Ads Troubleshooting

Common Facebook Ads issues and how to troubleshoot them

Chapter 9: Conclusion

Recap of key points

Final thoughts on Facebook Ads and Automation.

In this book, we will explore the world of Facebook Ads and Automation, and how you can use these powerful tools to grow your business. We will start with the basics of Facebook Ads, including the different types of ads and how to set up a Facebook Ads account. From there, we will move on to creating effective Facebook ads, including strategies for creating compelling ad copy and visuals

Prologue

Scaling and Expanding Facebook Ad Campaigns

Chapter 7: Facebook Ads Case Studies

Examples of successful Facebook Ad campaigns

Analysis of the strategies used in each campaign

Chapter 8: Facebook Ads Troubleshooting

Common Facebook Ads issues and how to troubleshoot them

Chapter 9: Conclusion

Recap of key points

Final thoughts on Facebook Ads and Automation.

In this book, we will explore the world of Facebook Ads and Automation, and how you can use these powerful tools to grow your business. We will start with the basics of Facebook Ads, including the different types of ads and how to set up a Facebook Ads account. From there, we will move on to creating effective Facebook ads, including strategies for creating compelling ad copy and visuals

CHAPTER ONE

In this book, we will explore the world of Facebook Ads and Automation, and how you can use these powerful tools to grow your business. We will start with the basics of Facebook Ads, including the different types of ads and how to set up a Facebook Ads account. From there, we will move on to creating effective Facebook ads, including strategies for creating compelling ad copy and visuals

www.ingramcontent.com/pod-product-compliance
Lightning Source LLC
Chambersburg PA
CBHW071315130726
47997CB00007B/2572